DOES LIFE GET ANY EASIER WHEN WE GET OLD?

DOES LIFE GET ANY EASIER WHEN WE GET OLD?

by

Donna Anita Bennett

ISBN: 979-8-218-32003-4

Cynthia

Gail

Denise

Lynn

Never be afraid of who you are. As you age, know that you have become a better version of yourself. And that you were able to live your life as intelligently as your brain would allow by staying healthy, growing, and continuing to learn whatever was placed in front of you, and that you were not afraid to say, "I couldn't be better when asked how you were feeling today!"

TABLE OF CONTENTS

PROLOGUE

Having a five-year plan to navigate my way into retirement was a huge help to me back in October 2004. I realized that I had to live within my means, but the good thing about that was that I had always been a saver. I had managed my money well; when I got my social security check and my pension, I would pay myself first.

I learned to use this method: "Is it a want or a need? Anything that has a need is a must, but a want is a once-a-month gift to myself." And yes, that worked for me. We all have our very own stories to tell; however, each of us has a unique tale to share; I'm just sharing mine.

Chapter One
THIS IS MY STORY

I call this story *Does Life Get Any Easier When We Get Old?* Let's discuss it. I'm seventy-five years old, and wow, this has opened my eyes. These days, I find myself thinking aloud more often. I therefore composed this book with my siblings in mind when I sat down to write it.

When we were young, we were wholesome and content, with a lot of vigor and involvement in our activities. Oh yes, we had so much energy that we could accomplish anything. Even after having our own children, there was always that sense of contentment that we had nothing to worry about. We were overflowing with love for life. Guess what? As we got older, life took a turn and slowed down. We were all filled with the love of life.

As we grew older, life started to fade away from us in a mysterious way, without even saying goodbye. Since life and the value of love were always the keys, I can never forget the intense affection that was held in our family. In addition, whether you believe it or not, life and love really go hand in hand.

Living life to the fullest kept us united in that connection, which was based primarily on love at that time. However, life has gradually dwindled as we all appear to be approaching our late seventies and early eighties. What do you know? I simply refuse to let it lead me in that direction. I'm still trying to figure out why things happen in life. Life—what is it? How does one process that thought? Is slumber regarded as a lack of existence?

In order to view life as it truly ought to be seen, I have a few questions. Let's start by discussing the meaning of life: is it something that moves and breathes, or is it viewed as a give and take? I may need to take a step back and consider the development of life, but I'm going to try and process it. What, in general, makes a person satisfied with their life? It will also take me a moment to comprehend that. Life is defined by the Oxford Dictionary as the condition of being alive and the capacity of humans, animals, and plants to breathe, grow, reproduce, etc. Perhaps if I look up the definition of *life* on Google, I could get something like this: Any system that is able to carry out processes like feeding, digesting, breathing, moving, developing, producing, and reacting to outside stimuli is considered alive.

What is life's actual purpose? My opinion on that question is that no one is truly able to define what it means to have a life. Some definitions say that life is all about happiness and building a family, while others may just leave life as it is, having no worries at all about it or its departure. For some, it's about accumulating wealth, whereas for others, it's all about love. What are your true thoughts about that?

Life is what it is when you live your best life in ways that will make you happy and successful in finding your way. As you find peace in your surroundings, producing a sure way of living and enjoying ageless time here on this earth. I'm thinking out loud; for some reason, the mind needs to stay focused on something that you love on a daily basis.

I do believe that as we get older, we forget a lot of things, not to say that young people always remember. When my daughter and I are having tea together, I can sometimes tell by the look on her face that I might be repeating myself; I seem to be doing that a lot lately. But she always lets me know by reframing and not saying a thing. Do you believe she should say something if she's heard it before?

I'll give you two examples. My two amazing children approach listening to me very differently; they both are wonderful people. One child would pay attention, then react if I repeated myself in any way, letting me know that they had indeed heard me say it before. The other, however, would just brush it off as if it were something they had never heard before.

When my husband and I had our children, we loved them with all our hearts and without conditions. It has been a joy knowing that these two have been there for their mother without reservation since the passing of their father. It has been a priceless gift. It's been said that if we take care of our children, later in life our children in some form will care for their parents.

Is it true that, as we get older, we go through a second childhood? Is that when dementia and Alzheimer's develop? Someone, please raise your hand and tell us something about that question. As I've gotten older, my eyes have been on the prize, and that prize has been keeping my brain going. I believe that through my daily writing, it has continued to shape my thinking, keeping me above water, so to speak.

I do have that fear, as everyone believes that when the brain or mind is lost, there is nowhere else to go with your life as you get older. So I'm going to write every day as a teaching tool for my mind and brain to stay healthy. Do you ever take some time to think about your own preferences in life? What actually keeps you going and makes you happy? I was told that I was born on a Friday.

I remember my grandmother's jewelry box having a nursery rhyme on it, and she would sit by the window and read it. I would walk into the room, where I heard her reading that nursery rhyme out loud: "Monday's child is fair of face; Tuesday's child is full of grace; Wednesday's child is full of woe; Thursday's child has far to go; Friday's child is loving and giving; Saturday's child works hard for her living; and the child that is born on a Sunday is bonny and blithe and good and happy." That beautiful nursery rhyme has stuck with me for many years. I had a plaque made of it for my children.

My daughter was born on a Sunday, and my son on a Friday. It helped them to know the days of the week, enhance their character, and shed some light on their future.

My favorite plaque is "Children Learn What They Live" by Dorothy Law Nolte. It would be a wonderful experience if every parent could place this in their children's rooms.

This was always a good teaching source for my two. That was how I raised them—by reading this to them every chance I got when entertaining their bedrooms. Allow me to share this priceless piece by Dorothy Law Nolte.

Take a minute and read through, and you will truly see clearly and understand what I mean. This would benefit so many of our children today. In today's world, I do believe that a large number of our children are being educated by social media, along with many other forms of distraction. That has taken away the joy of being a child, a teen, or a mature adult in our world today.

Tell me—what are your thoughts about this priceless piece? Would you want this for your grandchildren to be placed on the wall in their room as well? This has been a practical resource for my children, and it has helped them become effective and better adults in this troubling society of today.

My family's presence at the dinner table meant the world to me; we would hold family conversations and keep a close eye on their activities. They would invite their friends over for dinner, so we could get to know them. We made sure that their friends felt comfortable when opening up to us about any personal concerns, and we were always concerned about how they were doing academically.

However, go ahead and read the next page.

Children Learn What They Live
by Dorothy Law Nolte

If children live with criticism, they learn to condemn.
If children live with hostility, they learn to fight.
If children live with fear, they learn to be apprehensive.
If children live with pity, they learn to feel sorry for themselves.
If children live with ridicule, they learn to feel shy.
If children live with jealousy, they learn to feel envy.
If children live with shame, they learn to feel guilty.
If children live with encouragement, they learn confidence.
If children live with tolerance, they learn patience.
If children live with praise, they learn appreciation.
If children live with acceptance, they learn to love.
If children live with approval, they learn to like themselves.
If children live with recognition, they learn it is good to have a goal.
If children live with sharing, they learn generosity.
If children live with honesty, they learn truthfulness.
If children live with fairness, they learn justice.
If children live with kindness and consideration, they learn respect.
If children live with security, they learn to have faith in themselves and in those around them.
If children live with friendliness, they learn the world is a nice place in which to live.

You would undeniably concur that it's a fantastic piece of art. So as we proceed to discover fulfillment in our second journey as seniors, we make an effort to give the archives of memories that our minds have stored this particular time in our lives top priority.

Whenever I stop to check the clock, I am amazed at how fast it appears to be going by. Days are passing by so quickly that it's becoming more and more difficult to keep track of time. Whoa! Time waits for no one or nothing anymore. Is it possible that you may already sense the arrival of the next day, but it will pass quickly, much like a thief in the night? A day consists of twenty-four hours. It always seems like there are fewer hours in a day, as my memory serves me correctly.

Sometimes I'm extremely good at managing time, and other times I just don't know. What has been your quest for making time work for you?

The other day I met my neighbor in the store; although it had been a while since seeing one another, we stopped to chat and catch up. She shared some news about her neighbor next door, who had just suddenly developed dementia, and how her husband had to make some changes.

As we get older, dementia and other old-age diseases find their way into our lives. It must be difficult for that neighbor and his wife to make a change and continue to live their best lives in the manner they were used to. I wonder if it has anything to do with not being more active that allows dementia to find an opening to come in. Or is it hereditary?

Truth be told, not every old person will develop dementia or some of the other old-age diseases. I try to stay busy, and by all means, try to center yourself around some young ones. I know that it sounds funny when some young people think that we are too old to be around their kind.

Nope! While the young ones should give it some thought and think maybe they can learn something on the same coin, as seniors we can learn quite a lot from the younger generations as well.

Chapter Two

TRYING TO MAKE SENSE OF EVERYTHING

When I initially retired in 2009, after applying for and receiving my resources, I remember how bizarre it was to no longer go to work yet still receive a paycheck. I applied for social security and received a pension check, but only if you qualified for one. When you depart from employment with a company, your employer will guarantee an income for you as a pension. You had to work for an employer for a predetermined number of years in order to receive your pension benefits.

With each additional year of service with that employer, your pension benefit typically increases. A person must now buy into or choose to have a pension today.

Here's something funny I remember thinking about while out and about and feeling excited about being retired. I was getting up every day with no work, and then it came to me: What if they forget to deposit that social security check or pension? I would be devastated, for sure. What if that system doesn't work now that I'm finally retired?

With these questions, how was I going to pay a few bills if nothing showed up in my bank account? I knew that I had my savings to fall back on and some other tucked-away investments, but still, this left me a bit worried because this was all so new for me to take in.

Then again, I felt that I was cheating the system because I wasn't working. I felt guilty. I had some strange thoughts, but all in all, it all worked out. Checks don't fail me now, as I continue to feel elated as I receive my Social Security and pension right on time every month.

I can remember approximately six years before I retired, when I started my five-year plan. I'm so glad I did. Everything worked out well. I found myself wanting to share the idea of getting your plans together with some friends, but they were not interested at all; however, it was their loss in getting ahead for that big day.

I had developed a five-year plan five years before I set out to retire. I paid off every credit card and all bills, and I bought no new items for five years and saved every cent. I would watch my spending, having only these words to live by every day: *Is it a want or is it a need?*

So being able to save and purchase only what I needed throughout those five years was the motivation that got me to a good place when I retired.

To tell the truth, I enjoyed the work that I did after leaving the company. The fact of the matter was that the company gave out an awesome buyout to those who were eligible at the time. Some employees who were close to retirement age opted to take the package and leave as well. That was so clever of me to get started on that five-year plan, all because it was so very helpful in the end.

Coming out at sixty-one with all my credit paid off, no bills, and a comfortable mortgage was right on time when I accepted the package from the company. However, it was still kind of scary at first after being programmed for so many years to wake up at 5:30 a.m. The best part of all of this was that, for the first week, I felt as if I was not needed.

Once I settled into some retirement time, maybe a month later, I tried to get in touch with some coworkers who had been left behind because they did not have the age and years of service to qualify for retirement. It was difficult at that time to keep in touch with them and other coworkers, all because we now had different journeys to travel through.

They were meeting deadlines, and I was taking on mini-day trips and other activities. On that note, I slowly but surely got away from trying to connect with past acquaintances after working so many years together. So now one can find solace when going to the post office, the market, the train station, the doctor's office, and with your family and friends that are now outside of your workplace.

I find myself meeting nice people along the way in my daily life as I go out and about. I want to say that this has been my season to grow in wisdom and peace of mind. I've been retired now for going on fourteen years, and surely I have grown.

When I finally reached the age of sixty-five, I thought I had it all figured out until I took on Medicare and secondary insurance. Not wanting to pay out of pocket, I found that my medical was sky high in price and became a very expensive deduction.

You see, for seniors, a good rule of thumb is that we have to start eating the right foods, exercising, staying active, and knowing our numbers. We must try hard to stay healthy in order to beat the high cost of our medical care.

Meaning, stay on top of your blood work and know those numbers. Can you say that you know your numbers? Choose to put some time into exercising every day and stay active. If you have a computer, use it to do some research to improve your health and find a passion that will make you happy. Eat a healthy breakfast, learn to juice, and make better meal choices.

The art of being knowledgeable about going into my senior years was very important to me because I had stepped into a new kind of journey. I've learned a lot of new things along the way, and I've learned to love myself. Look into your mirror and take the time to pat yourself on the back as you complete every new project, activity, and experiences that you continue to take on.

Life has given me everything I need to push forward as I age on its timeline, all because I want to keep going and maintain the skills to continue to excel in everything I set out to do. Living is so important in finding that light to get you through those aches and pains on a daily basis, so you can learn to keep smiling and push as hard as you can to stay relevant as you age with a smile. And yes, it can be done, because I am the living proof.

There's a saying that goes something like this: "Never let your left hand know what the right hand is doing." But pardon me for changing that and allowing both hands to work together. Essential tremors are no joke, and they can become very debilitating at times, making it difficult to carry on with your everyday activities.

I remember my first bout with ET at age fifty-two. Check it out. Would you kindly have a look at it? It would make a little more sense to you. It's not Parkinson's, although some people believe that might be what a person has while looking across the table at a restaurant.

I cannot emphasize enough how important it is for me to continue to live my best life, accomplish everything I want, and not look at myself as incapable of doing the things I love.

I have become an Eveready battery, like back in the day, that keeps going and going.

I'm simply saying that some days you may think you've got it bad until you see that person who isn't able to talk, walk, or even get out of bed, but you did that day. You just have to learn to push harder each day to get through.

Remember, it's totally okay to seize the moment by being honest when you are not well. Try not to keep that moment in mind while continuing to feel bad but looking on the bright side. Better days will come. Since moving from the east coast and living in sunny Arizona, I've never felt better; in fact, I feel good every day. The sun here does me good, and besides, the cooler season here is something to be grateful for at all costs.

Some senior recreation centers can be helpful as we get older to mingle with folks there to learn new kinds of activities. Yoga places are nice for seniors to partake in. I definitely would not advise the seniors to get hooked on going to the casino; they should come with a responsible adult.

I visit the casino twice a year, and of course I win, not all the time but most of the time. I have seen seniors get drained dry trying to get their money back from those machines. It's a sport. Have fun and know your limit. Go have dinner in one of the nicer restaurants or see a show. The point is to find a passion and invest in it, for sure, and you can fulfill your days by living some quality moments.

Know what you can and cannot do on your own; ask for help with those things, and never feel that you just can't make it possible.

Leave something for your children and grandchildren to admire, and be passionate about what you accomplished before leaving this world. Don't wait for things to happen; as long as you're in the right frame of mind, you can make things happen.

Block out any and all the fears that are limiting your ability to move forward and conquer everything at your age. I know that people stay on point while saying that age is only a number. That number really gets bigger every year.

Yet when we were young at heart, we couldn't wait to turn sixteen, eighteen, and finally twenty-one years old. I remember how, after that time, I was unstoppable from saying anything more. Jeepers creepers—when you look around and see how time has flown by you finally realize that you are now fifty years old and signing up for AARP magazine. Oh, tell me about that. I had to laugh at myself when I started identifying myself as a senior at sixty-two and later found out that—oops!—not quite yet could I be considered a senior; society labels sixty-five and up as your newly arrived senior journey.

Don't you just love it now that Medicare has popped into the picture?

Seriously, I'm laughing so far because my journey has had a lot of good twists and turns, growth, development, and excitement. Oh, yes, let's not forget about the wisdom of finding a way for you to share.

Getting older has a way of allowing you to go first in some cases, as people look at the aging quality or lines you may have grafted on your face. Example: Excuse me, please let the seniors move up front or let them go first.

Then again, I never allow anything to worry or bother me anymore because, to me, life is so short, and I appreciate every moment, whether difficult or just okay! You see, life is what you make of it.

By that, I mean I awake every day at 6:00 a.m., and it has been extremely beneficial for me to use my treadmill, take my medications, drink my fresh glass of lemon water, and then have my hot cup of clove tea.

My favorite sit-down time is at my computer, sipping a peaceful cup of tea. I have been doing the intermittent fast long before I really knew what that meant.

Eating one meal a day and having that be my biggest meal at 2:00 p.m. has been a healthy way for me to enjoy my daily intake of a healthy meal.

I can tell you that my daily intake consists of lots of fresh fruits and vegetables. Later, maybe I'll have a cup of soup and half a sandwich, or maybe some fresh fruit.

I have no secrets other than that I am a woman of a particular age, and now, at seventy-six, I can tell you that I am indeed living my best life. I weigh exactly 134 pounds. While my height is 5'2," now my primary doctor has given me notice that I am now shrinking a bit.

As we get older, there's some shrinkage, and I'm still laughing because life, as long as we are still here, will have its funny moments. To tell the truth, isn't laughter labeled as a form of medicine that one can offer another as the form of healing? I know that laughter does me a lot of good, and I have some every day with family and friends. Just a dose a day will do the job. What do you think?

There's so much in life to be thankful for as we age; just look around and know that as long as you get up every day, a lot can be said about that as far as being relevant and alive.

Chapter Three

LEARNING HOW TO TAKE CARE OF OURSELVES

Learning how to take care of ourselves can be a bit scary now that we are older. It becomes more about our ability, activity, and energy level, and I could go on. Well, you know, sometimes I find myself talking out loud in reference to my body changes: having wrinkles and dry skin, developing saggy breasts and arms, and not being able to make a fist because of the arthritis in my hands; this causes frustration.

I never allow that to make me take a backseat. And also, it becomes a celebration as we see what comes next, because these changes come with age. I continue to push forward and enjoy the things that make me happy while I'm still here, enjoying my life to the fullest, always with a smile.

As we live our lives, everything wears out, and we dread the thought of aging or getting old. It catches up to you, whether you are ready or not, so you might as well accept the fact that life is a give and take.

Life gives you a means to live your life to the fullest, yet when you reach a certain age or not, life can be taken away, and this can happen to anyone. It takes our lives back and gives us what God knows in return. Things like missing a step and breaking a hip, being on too many medications, causing early dementia, not taking proper care of our eyes and going blind, smoking, drinking, eating poorly, not having a proper diet, and now you find out that you have cancer, especially when it's not curable, and then you're dead. Yep!

You're done, and with no proper healing time at all, because when sickness strikes, it comes with a vengeance, hitting every organ. Like a thief in the night, it will steal your entire life in the blink of an eye. As much as I work on myself to stay beautiful inside and out, I love life and owe everything to the Most High and the Universe.

I've never learned to walk on eggshells; being a conscientious person, I learned to be in favor of all the challenges that life had in store for me. Criticism was always unfavorable to me; however, encouragement gave me all kinds of love as one of the stepping stones to pushing forward and making a much better life by taking care of me. I would critique myself at times, allowing it to be my method of discipline.

Although it's commonly understood as fault-finding, it becomes a negative way to judge, but it allows me to recognize my own merits. However, right now, as a woman of a particular age, I've paid my dues and know nothing else but to embrace my life every day.

As I awake in the early morning, I look out my bedroom window, where the sun is always shining brightly, giving me the best "Grand Rising" wishes ever. Living here in Arizona is breathtaking, along with its daily dose of sunshine. The mountains are amazing, giving me that first healthy kick of the day. As my days continue to be approachable, it allows me to have a new page in my life so that I can wear it with a smile to the end of each day.

And to think that life and love surround me like a halo, shining a light so bright that it directs my path while I place one foot in front of the other, makes me appreciate all that is given in my life today.

I don't take anything for granted—nope, not anymore. I absorb and inhale everything that is good coming from our Universe. I really try to eat what is healthy and what I need to keep my body totally nourished on a daily basis.

As a senior, I find that the body is not the same, especially the digestive system, which can be out of whack. What really is a good meal for those women in their seventies? Why doesn't everyone respond so fast and all at the same time? Listen, I'm ready to raise my hand and answer that question.

No one can really give you the truth or an honest answer, because no one really knows; maybe because everyone's body at seventy is different, what fits me may not be the right way of eating for you. Look around you; check out the world we live in: the fast food chains, the farms having bad luck with crops, the food contamination, and the population that has grown.

I've heard that some seniors are not able to purchase nutritious foods for their bodies that would be considered affordable. Everything is sky-high in price. As a senior, you have to give up something to get something. For example, instead of purchasing your medications this month, you may have to forfeit them to pay a much-needed bill.

There's so much going on about our foods that America refuses to tell us, just so money can be made with every purchase. No one really gives a damn about life anymore. It's the time we live in. If you had to survive on just water, would you be able to survive on clean water alone?

In today's world, our water is loaded with harmful chemicals, even bottled water do not use the best springs. Everyone is trying to pocket money, even if it means producing their own and labeling it as the best water. So again, what foods would allow seniors to achieve the longevity of a more healthy lifestyle? I love to walk every day, which is a good way of exercising, and it's my right to say I've worked out. Walking thirty to forty minutes a day works in my favor, and it works well for me.

I call it my full-body workout, and I drink about four sixteen-ounce bottles of water a day. Drinking lots of water is a good habit to get into, because it keeps your entire body constantly lubricated if you drink it every day. Water is absolutely a good source of energy as well.

In fact, it has become my favorite beverage. Having a glass of water and adding a piece of fruit or sliced cucumber makes your drink so delightful. I've learned how to drink more natural fruit and vegetable juices, along with delicious smoothies.

A good walk allows me to open up to my God and the Universe by having a conversation from the heart. Keeping your hands clean is very important.

It will prevent you from getting sick and spreading germs to yourself and others. As a senior, I find that it can be so easy to forget the simple but important things to do to keep your body safe from germs. Many diseases and conditions are spread by not washing hands with soap and clean water. Breakfast is the first meal of the day, but sometimes I find myself so full of spiritual food that I'm not yet hungry for my breakfast, so I will read something that will lift my spirits even more.

I enjoy writing; it's free and easy, and it has been very stimulating and calming for me. Living in Arizona, I find that the weather is the best, and each day is better than the day before.

I mean, I've had nothing but good days every day. It's because I finally took charge of my life after the loss of my dear friend. I promised myself to stay true to what my friend and I had vowed to do before his passing.

We never lost sight of what we both believed in, because we loved each other unconditionally. Life with love works together, and if anything should happen to him, I'd promised to hang on to my joy, and his thoughts proved to be the same; to hang on unconditionally as well.

Stay focused on the best quality life has to offer, and know that at this time, someone will be coming into your life for a lifetime. Stay present around family and good friends.

Make yourself a better version of yourself for that once-in-a-lifetime friend who is out there waiting to find you.

My dear friend Daniel would call me Sweetea; he would simply say, "I want someone to find you as the love of their life one day when I leave this earth. There's much more happiness waiting for you, because I already know the joy in loving you in the way you carry yourself, your thoughtfulness, your bright smile, and the grace that you carry around, making you so beautiful as my phenomenal woman. I've been blessed so highly, and I know that God's plans are masterpieces, and because God already knows our story, God is going to bless you with a phenomenal man. In him, you will feel my presence, indicating that he is the one that is meant to put that balance in your remaining time on earth."

Chapter Four

WHAT HAPPENS IF I SHOULD FALL ASLEEP?

What happens if I should fall asleep and never awake? Let's talk about that in this chapter. Is there such a thing as a wake-up call? One morning, as I took some time to slowly get up and inhale the precious gift of seeing another beautiful day, it dawned on me that life is not guaranteed. I've never thought about life in that way, but that day was when it all became real.

We're here today, and within the same day, life can be taken away, meaning that death is inevitable. The dictionary defines it as the passing away, the end of life, or the permanent destruction of something. At that very moment, my thoughts became real about how easy it would be to slip out of sight and be no more of me, so this gave me a wake-up call.

What if there were no more of me? As fate has it, we are not given nine lives at birth. Truth be told, do cats really have nine lives? Just because cats always land on their feet, it's an inspiring thought to think we all would love to do the same. However, we are given only one life to live, and if we blow that by allowing it to become our fault or whatever happens, then we're done.

I'm trying to learn to live a better life each day; at least every day is filled with gratitude and a challenge. And nothing is personal, but when we leave this earth, things are left behind, and ownership is gone. And you no longer exist, but memories are left on a shelf, and that too will evaporate as time passes.

That's when these three questions came to mind as clearly as the day seemed long: What is life? What is the absence of life? What does it mean to be gone and vanished from this life?

Well, my interpretation of life begins first with a thought; then the seed is planted, which gives life, entitlement, and existence. Life then gives you the surroundings that will allow growth and development to take place. By any means necessary, you then find yourselves in a universe where the voices of the human race, known as mankind, are present.

I strongly see the absence of life as a lack of presence. And lastly, to be gone and vanished from life is when your existence is taken away, never to be returned to your original state of mind and body.

Obviously, death is always at the center of our lives, whether we know it or not, and that's for sure.

No matter where you are or what you may be doing, it will always find you.

It will find a way to take your spirit, leaving you with the shell of a body to be disposed of. In the meantime, your soul will leave and find its way home to a much better place to live forever. Tell me what is meant when we say "forever." Is there such a place to be seen that has been noted as a place of paradise to live forever? I find it hard to believe that no one has returned from their death experience—I mean, for those people who have been absent for years.

What if they could bring back with them the good news of actually speaking and seeing loved ones and listening to their stories? They would be able to come back and tell family and friends about that encounter. It has been said that those people have seen bright lights, angels, and images of their God, but more is needed in order to tell a great story of where you've been in that forever place called paradise, known as heaven. With no pun intended, let's use the word *absence* instead of the word *death.*

I guess it would be nice if the soul could check out heaven first, then come back to life with God's approval and reunite with the body to maybe stay on earth.

It would be so nice to stay awhile once you have seen this place, namely, a paradise, in order to get a good feeling about heaven.

Or maybe you would want to stay there forever instead of coming back to family and friends, because you have found some peace. That's just a crazy thought, nothing more. Of course, not all souls will go to heaven. I do believe that there's another place that has been talked about that is not so nice. It's believed to be a place of torture. Some think that place is here on earth. What do you think?

I really think that some people are accurate in how they live their lives, as they see their torments right here on earth.

It has to be a higher source that gives permission to the spirit to call on your soul for a ticket to leave the body. A loss of a loved one is heartbreaking, as always, as we leave family, loved ones, and friends behind.

In general, we all share a sense of broken hearts, as our days are busy. It's strictly inevitable that each of us has a turn to enter the state of absence's door, as our number will one day be called.

I often think as thoughts go. Will I be afraid of death when it comes looking for me? I don't know, but I will tell you this: I will be ready.

I believe the most uncommon fear is not knowing who will escort you home to that beautiful paradise in heaven. In all essence, and for honesty's sake, will you recognize all of your family and friends that have gone before you?

Here's some food for thought; just think about it for a minute.

Or will it take some much-needed time for me or you to get acclimated to the system of things, especially when entering another place and time? No one has ever come back to share their thoughts on this unknown place, and some say it's a better place after you're gone.

However, many have confirmed, through their own version of a vision, what heaven is really like. Some have stated that there's beauty in leaving your body as your soul enters a new journey, while others see their version of their own vision as quite different. I have no idea; all I know is that I'll have to wait until my turn comes in order to see for myself and determine my own version of my vision.

At seventy-six years old—or should I say seventy-six years young—I find myself very pensive in my thoughts when it comes to quiet moments alone. And more at times, because I still miss my friend and companion. We did everything possible together.

He was a good man, an extraordinary person with a good heart. I have to smile when I say "with a good heart," because if he had such a good heart, why was it his time to leave this earth? Allow me to share something. We don't realize that whatever sickness we have in life, we die of that illness. But that is not so; it has always been the heart's intention to take you out first and foremost every time.

For example, if a person has cancer, kidney disease, or a fatal bullet wound, it's always the heart that gives out; honestly, the heart takes you out. Once that heart stops beating, you are done, and you are no more—you're absent. That means you're done.

It must have been my dear friend's time to move on and leave things behind; we all have our times documented in the books of life and death by our amazing creator, and by all means, let's be clear. The Most High has everything under control.

It's so not obvious that, at birth, we are born with an indelible mark embossed somewhere on our bodies, and we have no idea that it exists. Yet as quiet as it's kept, the Most High holds all the records. Are you still with me?

Then allow me to explain why I felt sad but not at all depressed when I lost my best and dearest friend, whom I loved unconditionally. For several days, I cried a lot, because I truly missed his presence.

I got lost in my own world of grief, which kept me tied up in knots. It wore me out with a heaviness that I held in my heart which drained my health. Of course, my heart was not broken, and that meant that it was very repairable, vibrant, and strong.

All because of the strong armor of love we had for each other, I was able to conquer the biggest job: not giving up in any way for my heart to lose sight of having lost a love that could never again be found in order to find love again when it was time.

My heart had to go through therapy, and what didn't break it made it stronger. One thing is that I made a decision to find peace by remembering the love we both shared and how nothing could allow that feeling to expire.

Now, as time moves forward and the years pass, will it then be my time to say goodbye to life as well? So for now, my friend is in a better place, even though no one has ever seen this "better place," no one has literally come back to tell us about such a place.

I can only assume there is comfort in all of this, as we use the term *in a better place* to allow the soft side of keeping things simple, and short of that, life continues to go on. With the strength and love of my faith, I trust God and the Universe to see me through when my time arrives for this journey.

Now, as the days continue to slowly go by, I'm finding more things about myself that I should have known. As a woman of an appropriate age, and how loneliness would be interpreted in my life in ways that it would give or take away from finding joy and happiness, along with me getting to know myself at this particular age now.

I like what I see in myself; I never get tired of growing, learning, and having more time to love myself, to become a better me for someone who will light up my life with unconditional love once again. I never give up on love or relationships, no matter how old I realize that I am. I know in my heart that there is someone out there for me. I now realize that people come into your life for a reason, a season, or a lifetime.

And when my best friend came into my life, I realized that it was meant for a season. Those seasons gave me a birth of knowledge on how two people interpret life in living and learning so much about each other.

While learning how to compromise, work together, understand old age, pain, and hurt, along with the sadness and gladness in everything that exists for the both of us. We discovered that laughter was the best kind of medicine and always gave us a sure cure. Along with the smiles we shared daily, that was the seal of approval.

In life, we are not promised a rose garden; however, throughout my life, I have created my own beautiful floral garden. The many friendships throughout my life helped to maintain an imaginary garden with so many colored roses. We are born into a world with a revolving door; birth and death have to work together as easily as give and take, up and down, open and close, right and wrong, and so many other variations that must work together to make sense.

My belief is that people come into the world at birth with a book that opens once they're born. And life allows them to breathe; their book is then opened to the first page of their life story to be told as God sees them, and then it is recorded.

Stay with me now. Have you ever had a procedure done?

It's like waiting for the cows to come home for your results, which at times can be so draining and life-deprived. But for the doctor, he's simply doing his job because, as protocol goes, doctors are never working alone.

There are many skilled professionals along the way who have their jobs to do for the doctor to determine your diagnosis. Sometimes the results are positive; then they may be negative, but during that time, life still goes on. So you learn to make the best of it. Yet life continues to move forward as you live your life to the fullest, leaving nothing to the imagination as to where it will take you. You continue to thrive on what you know will give you balance and make you happy.

Chapter Five

STAY WITH ME NOW

I seriously hope that I'm not repeating myself; you all know by now that I am a senior as well. Okay, can we talk about it? I'm sure you all have something to say; don't everyone jump up at the same time to share their opinion.

Isn't it strange how some of us seniors become feisty, mean, and just not comfortable being around other seniors? I used to think that maybe they were in some kind of pain, hurting, or unhappy in some way so that it would bother them to see other healthy, bright, smiling faces in their way. How sad that sounds!

Do we all have that kind of range at times?

What really brings us down when we begin to develop a selfish spirit that allows us to be unhappy? Can anyone explain that? Here's the deal. I have to laugh out loud every time I say those words, because, as one of my friend would say to me, it sounds like you're setting up a heist for something to go down.

I'm still laughing because I made a promise to myself to watch my words.

Okay! So let's get back to what I was saying. My opinion is that the brain plays tricks that cause confusion that some seniors are afraid to share, and this causes a fear that something is wrong, and being around those that seem to be okay may cause strife to show through.

Think about it. What's your opinion?

My friend was the nicest person that I could ever be so lucky to have. One day he was watching *The Price is Right* on TV, and the volume was so high. He said he couldn't hear it; that was the reason he turned it up. Then I realized that the TV was turned up too high, and I always found myself turning it down. Later, we found out that it wasn't that he couldn't hear the television or radio; it was that he lost the ability to understand the words that were being said.

And that too may be a reason for some seniors to be feisty, mean, and not likeable. Would I find something similar taking place in my aging experiences? Well, I think I'll learn how to adjust my TV so that I can have the closed caption display available, and that does make life easier.

Please continue to stay with me, and don't get me wrong. I'm not trying to say that it has been uncomfortable living my life as a senior. I'm only telling myself and all those who find it interesting that it becomes a journey as we grow older. And the things we do now are much different from what we did back then. Imagine this: if you live to be one hundred years old, do you think telling your story of how you got to that age could help others? My guess is that if you don't watch out for yourself when you find yourself getting older, then how do you expect to do the same things that got that person to reach that age?

It starts early in life with you wanting to live to your rightful age and taking good care of yourself in order to accomplish that.

Here's a funny story. My neighbor's husband had been smoking for forty-six years straight, and he loved every bit of his time going outside to smoke. He would even rush his breakfast and dinner times to be able to go outside to smoke his cigarette. She would tell me that he had never smoked in their home; however, she was getting sick and tired of his smoking altogether. One day both she and I met at Trader Joe's.

We did some small talk, and the conversation went into discussing her husband and how she had finally decided to ask him to stop smoking.

And then she stated, He said, "Only God can make me stop." A week later, she said, he had a heart attack.

"Oh, my" was my response to that, and then she continued to say, "Well, now my husband has stopped smoking for good."

What's so funny about this story is that it's not funny; it becomes food for thought as we continue to not care about our health, and the truth be told, God really does listen, and I'm sure that he hears what we say when we cry out.

At that point, I did believe her husband wanted to stop but didn't know how to stop his addiction or felt okay about seeking some kind of help because of his age. Getting old or becoming older does not limit on your ability to learn more things as you age. I've been open to learning many new things as I go along; in fact, as seniors, we must learn to embrace the thought of discovering something new.

If you enjoy writing poems, do yourself a favor by creating a short book of your poetry, or maybe if you enjoy love stories or some fantasy stuff, go for it and do something extraordinary. I love homemade soap, and I know a woman who lives not too far from me who enjoys that craft, and yes, she's seventy-six years old. There are so many productive seniors living their dreams as we speak, which means life keeps going as long as you're in the circle of existence in a world with so many opportunities, no matter what age category you're in.

And with that being said, what are you doing that has made a difference in your new journey? Are there dreams and aspirations that you want to accomplish while still living in this society? Sometimes we have to take a minute to look at ourselves in the mirror and question the idea that we are as old as we feel. What's that, you say?

Well, if I already know I'm old and I get up and feel old, am I still obligated to accomplish a task or two? Or would I get a free pass that allows me to sit and say, "I just cannot do it anymore?" If your brain serves you well, invest in a tape recorder and tell a piece of your positive life story.

You might have been a teacher and found out that you're just burned out. With nothing else but pure laziness to go on, don't do that to yourself. Have a reason to get up every day, knowing that you can live, love, and laugh while wearing your smile. My story has been all about simple things for simple folks living their best life and managing their time and money. Treat yourself; go on a staycation at a nice hotel, all lit up, and do absolutely nothing. Get dressed, go downstairs to the hotel dining area, and have a wonderful meal. You deserve that and more.

What retirement has meant for me is calculating my life differently, making my own standards for how I want to continue to live my life, and not having to work hard to get there. Scheduling a new wake-up time, eating earlier, finding a hobby, and planning and taking on some day trips that are affordable for you, as well as making all your doctor's appointments in the mornings and never having to be caught up in traffic and shopping while the stores are not overcrowded, allows you to find your way.

Dining out has become a pleasure, only because you can make reservations earlier and enjoy your meal.

Life has now become your resource haven by being more available and having some free time to do just about anything you want to do. When a dear friend of mine retired, I remember her saying, "I am enjoying my retirement because I'm doing absolutely nothing. I can get up when I want, and I don't have to hit the clock. It really feels good, and I'm going to sleep and watch TV all day and all night to make up for all the lost time when I was not able to do it." I thought, "Now what kind of retirement plan is that? And how is that a positive way to have a better quality of life?"

Don't lose yourself in the idea that retiring gives you the ability to have no life, so you shut down all the connecting outlets to keep you relevant in knowing how to live your life.

I know we all have different turning points in our lives as we grow older, and I'm not trying to put people down just because, after a certain age, they may deem themselves to have no more of a purpose in life.

I just want us to get up off that chair and dance, sing, and make some noise so everyone can hear that we couldn't be at all better as we head into the retirement process of living a better life.

You see, right now you can do your research, and yes, you may need to use your computer or go to the library and sit at one of the computers there and do some research.

If you want to walk but are afraid of walking alone, invest in a treadmill and start out with twenty to thirty minutes a day to get your exercise.

Then you have all the time in the world to do your research on what really is a healthy breakfast plan for your age. Lord knows I'm not looking down on those seniors who are loaded with serious health problems. They must follow their doctor's advice about taking it easy, having no stress, and not being made to do work that is harmful for them.

When I was fifteen years old, I became a candy striper in a geriatric nursing home. I felt bad because I wanted to be more helpful in assisting them. I couldn't understand why a lady there named Mrs. Lydia, who had been a retired schoolteacher, had to live there.

She wore these thick bottle-bottom glasses, and I thought that she could see because she didn't look old, until she said to me that she was blind. I guess it was because she was blind and had no family to care for her.

But she was the happy person there; it was her and her walking cane that directed her path wherever she needed to go in that home. While other folks there were very needy, my duties entailed feeding them, reading stories, and assisting those who were strong enough to walk to their bedroom or outside in the garden.

For me, it felt like this is what happened when you stopped working, and my impression from this is that you have to work all the time in order to stay young. Because as you get older, you would have to be living in a nursing home for someone other than your family to tend to your everyday needs and more.

Chapter Six

IS IT OKAY TO KEEP GOING?

Does life ever fascinate you when you look around and notice that a lot has changed and not everything stays the same?

And that leaves you hopeless, thinking that there's something new out there for you to try and keep going. And so what if you don't know? That would be the time to ask somebody. Don't hesitate to discover the new things that approach you that seem at first so difficult to understand. Know that it's okay to keep going and learning at the same time. I have a longtime friend who really made me realize how he gave up on being more knowledgeable at his age.

At only sixty-eight years old, he didn't want to ask anyone to assist him or help him with the apps on his cellphone. When asked about his new upgraded cellphone and how he enjoyed the convenience of having so much installed, his response was that he couldn't figure it out, and with a chuckle, he said, "I'm not smart enough to figure out all that technical stuff."

My first thought was, "Why would you purchase a phone with so much technical stuff?" Now, after several months, when I asked him again how he liked his cellphone, his statement was that he didn't want anyone to know that he had no skills in knowing how to access the information.

Dang, ask somebody. Sadly enough, he should have asked me; we had been friends for such a long time that there was no shame for him to fear. What do you think about that, and how would you have handled that situation?

Come on now, think about it, and give an outright positive answer on how you would have handled it. Tell me, does it seem as though I'm hard on people? I'm sorry if any of you think so. Situations like that sometimes bother me because we feel like, once we reach a certain age, we can give up on some things we were exploring only because we have no one to walk us through them.

As we begin reaching retirement age, we cut off a lot of what we used to do and what we enjoyed. It's true that maybe some senior folks enjoy sitting around, and just knowing that they are free from learning because of their age gives me the feeling that we lose interest in early retirement.

Retirement is when you leave your work life behind permanently, follow your own path, and enjoy a new life passion to achieve a better quality of life without having to work hard. On another note, some senior folks are reluctant to move out of state or try something new in order to test out some of the affordable senior communities.

When my daughter first moved out to live in Arizona, I couldn't see myself living there, mainly because the weather was always hot and dry. I had lived all my life on the east coast and had never thought of moving away from what I was used to. There would be no such thing as having four seasons anymore; I just loved the autumn trees and the beautiful snow when it would first fall and everything appeared as white as the snow.

Arizona was known for not having much rain but plenty to add to its monsoon seasons. And then what happened was that I would visit my daughter during the time I was working, and I would plan my vacation time to visit her twice a year. I learned to appreciate the sunshine, the palm trees, and the breathtaking sunrise and sunset.

Many things about Arizona began to touch my heart. And it has been a good haven for seniors as well. Really, the weather here is not so bad.

After my retirement a few years later, my decision was to move here permanently, and I'm glad I made that move. Would I ever go back to the east coast to live? Mmm, well, I will never say that I'm not going to ever go back to the east coast to live, but for right now, this is home for me.

One morning, while I was at the doctor's office, a patient was checking in with her information, and she seemed to be agitated about something. When she sat down next to me, we made eye contact and then shared a smile. She said, "They want me to give them more information than I can give; I'm not telling them everything because I don't know; I'm just old." My response to her was, "How old are you?"

She said, "I'm seventy-two years old." "Well," I said, "you're not old." (I said this to her because I was seventy-five and I believed that I was highly seasoned and not old yet.) "You really don't look your age. What is you secret?" I then smiled and said to her, I've learned to say these words: 'I couldn't be better,' when asked, 'How are you today?'

She responded, "On a day like this, when it is cloudy and rainy, I can only count six bones in my body that are okay."

She then introduced herself as Linda, with her hand stretched out.

We shook hands again as we gave each other a big smile. As I continued to wear my smile, I said to Linda, "You should try using these wonderful words—'I couldn't be better'—and see if you can bring out your healing spirit and see how you will find a positive way to shock those other bones into feeling so much better. Now that you've put it out into the universe, you can see and feel what will happen next."

Guess what? While Linda was waiting for her turn to see the doctor, she got my attention and said, "I'm going to do what you said and see if that really helps my spirit to stop complaining and be a better person for myself." A few minutes later, she was was called in to see her doctor; sometimes we're stopped along the way by people who want to express themselves by holding random conversations.

I wonder if those people saw a sign on that individual's forehead indicating that they wanted to talk or carry on a conversation. I understand that some of us do lose a small amount of interest in congregating with others, please don't get me wrong. I'm really a nice person, but why do some seniors find it difficult to have whole-hearted conversations, especially when having to get acquainted first?

I love bonding with my old friends, but sometimes it can be tough for a lot of us to meet new friends. As you can guess, as we get older, we get tired and easily disinterested in making a place or space for someone new to enter our lives when we have already lost many friendships.

It's so true that life goes on whether you like it or not, so why not meet people and create some fellowship while staying relevant and keeping up with what seniors enjoy doing as friends? You can learn to enjoy other people's company if you take the risk of visiting a senior recreation center near your area.

You can meet at the coffee shop, maybe have lunch, or you can always check out a movie. It can be rewarding when you have friends. It allows you to say that you had a wonderful day, and my life has some kind of balance because now I can look forward to learning and doing more things with people around my age that have some of the same interests. No one wants to sit around and not use their brain and shun people away.

Time is so precious, my dear, so get up off that chair and begin to understand what life is about.

I hope that I'm not boring you; this is the real deal. If you want to live your best life as a senior, get involved with life and the living. Every single day is a blessing, to say the least. Keep in mind that you got up and all of your functions are working and that someone else was not so lucky, and for your sake, wear your smile every day so that you don't create an automatic frown on your face.

Chapter Seven

EVERY DAY IS A MIRACLE

I truly believe that with every breath we take, we become that miracle. What are some of your beliefs? Can you say the same? Your heart plays an important part in keeping you filled with life in your body; if that gives out, all is lost.

Your job is to keep it running by staying active in a peaceful state and enjoying every moment that you are present. I'm not sure if I mentioned this before, but staying around some young people helps as well.

If living with your adult children gives you happiness because you have a daily presence with your grandchildren and you have become that voice of love and wisdom, you can surely embrace that and all that it has to offer.

I guess some of you are thinking, "What about the senior people who don't have children? They have no reason to be excited because they don't have any grandchildren." That's not so; those who don't have children or grandchildren will likely attract wonderful people into their lives who will treat them better than those who have children and grandchildren.

Then too many of the seniors live alone and manage to find peace, excitement, and adventure on their own. If that is so, more power to you, and I am so glad that you chose to make your own happiness by keeping your heart ticking. That makes me proud of you and your journey as a senior, because you refuse to sit around and have a pity party and allow life to pass you by.

Like that old saying says, you do what makes you happy, and then the best is yet to come because you cannot have it any other way as you learn to keep going.

We are living in a world with so much going on that politicians are somewhat hard to manage. Their morals have left the room. Many diseases are spreading around the world now, and disasters have found their way into every corner of the world.

Many seniors cannot make it on social security and pensions alone. However, truth be told, there are some seniors who are only receiving social security and who are still working to improve their lives by managing their daily responsibilities.

Believe me, trying to manage one's life financially to the fullest can really slow down a person's heart performance and bring on a heart attack or stroke.

Because in the world today, there's a lot to take in as far as living well. You see, in writing my story, I don't profess to be a doctor, lawyer, or someone in the ministry.

I'm simply sharing some tips and experiences that I felt that I wanted to share, and maybe you'll take something out of this book to give you a much better insight as to who you are and where you're going, as you see how I have learned to create some kind of purpose while still existing here in this world of fake and real opportunities.

It seems that as we get older, those opportunities do become a bit slimmer. What would you have to add? Come on, open up, and let's have some conversations to begin realizing that we all have a purpose, no matter what age. I kid you not when I say, "Let the fun begin," because none of us knows how long we have here. I only know that time flies by so fast and that time doesn't wait for anyone.

In a way, that has been my reason for not giving up my computer, so that I could stay connected and learn how to do my own research.

Even when I choose a doctor, I go online and check out his or her reviews. It also makes scheduling appointments and paying bills less stressful.

I really don't remember the last time I wrote out a check for something I needed or wanted. Have you ever tried ordering from Amazon or Instacart for anything? I upgrade my desktop computer every four or five years.

I upgrade my cellphone every three to four years as well. It's so nice to wake up every day with a clear head on your shoulders and know that you are still existing in a world with so much going on. I like to think that everyone should try to find peace and stillness as a way to be stress-free.

I have learned so much about myself these last few years since my dear friend passed away. Once or twice a year, I plan a staycation for myself. I make reservations at an affordable hotel and enjoy getting up and having some tea or coffee and a muffin, spending some time at the gym, sitting by the pool and enjoying a cool beverage, taking walks and checking out the shops and stores, getting casually dressed and having dinner even by myself, and always feeling a presence of enjoyment.

I guess it comes from being married for twenty-one years, finding a wonderful companion, and then, after almost twenty-two years, having to go through an unfortunate divorce. Then I prayed that God would send someone to me—not to take the person's place that I lost, but to fill the emptiness of not having someone in your life.

Then, about three years later, I started dating again, and every relationship that I ventured into was either for a season or, for whatever reason, never became a relationship for a lifetime. Oddly enough, I learned not to be anxious or overwhelmed by meeting new friends. It took so long until I did happen to meet someone special, and we managed to click and enjoy some of the same things.

We were together for about twelve years; he became the second love of my life until he was called home and departed from me, so now I take nothing for granted. For me, love is the moment you meet and begin a strong relationship, and learning how to embrace that love as we get older is important. I used to think that life wasn't fair, especially when you're at your happiest, because sometimes in life, something always and most surely will happen to disrupt that sound sign of finalized joy or happiness as it becomes that radiant sunshine that now has lit up your life.

And to think that a lifetime of happiness is possible—believe me, that will never happen in anyone's lifetime. That much I do know, and I can spend any amount of money on that notion. Because happiness doesn't last forever.

Nope! In this type of universe, real peace, joy, and happiness cannot be found in any relationship, only because we are all destined to die, and with that note, our happiness is destined to diminish for sure. Look, I don't mean to be drab or boring. Take a minute to think we live in a real world with many things happening on a daily basis.

I find myself not wanting to turn on the TV to watch the news. World news, of course, plays the part of telling nothing but problematic incidents and covering stories of shooting, murdering, robbing, and lastly, a one-minute good story to lift the spirits of the viewers. I know I'm simply getting a little ahead of myself, but going back to happiness after not being here for a lifetime is so true. Okay, then, what do you think?

Please be honest and realistic about the question. Are you in a relationship for life? We like to think we are, but we never know when it is time to leave this world.

So all I'm trying to tell you is to embrace and enjoy every moment with family, friends, and loved ones, and come on and realize that nothing lasts forever; there never was and never will be a lifetime relationship in our world. I'm going to remind you again that this is my story that I feel good about sharing, because everyone has their own opinion and beliefs and there are so many stories out there. My story is just one of them. I will leave you with this: we do have some everyday miracles that really take place in our world, despite all the distractions.

Right down the road from me, there was a lady who, from the back, looked like she was in her early fifties, and she came out with her water bottle and walked beside me. We had never met, and for the first time, we introduced ourselves as neighborly neighbors. Her name was Ms. Mattie, and when I looked at her face, she looked to be around seventy-nine or eighty, but she was holding on very strongly.

She had been in the same house for over thirty years, and she was on her way to play some pickleball with some senior friends. She was dressed in a short tennis-like outfit with white sneakers, and her hair was up in a ponytail. She did this every day at an indoor pickleball court.

I really admired her ambition as she strode along like she was no more than twenty-one years old. You see, now that's what I'm talking about. It takes all ages to enjoy a special quality of life, rather than depriving yourself, by staying young at heart, even at eighty. Oh, she did tell me that she was eighty-two. As we were walking toward the pickleball court, she said, "Would you like to join?"

And guess what? I'm now in love with pickleball, although I have seen quite a few seniors hurt while playing this sport. It's similar to tennis, I think, but it's different and new to us seniors, and so many are using the opportunity to play and stay in the game. Okay, since I have lived here, I have yet to meet a male companion just to say I have a friend. That's funny: when you're not looking, there's always someone out there who is always looking to find you.

And after living here for five years, I'm having the best time of my life, as every day has measured up to daily miracles. I say that because every day has been a "grand rising" moment. At any age, a person should learn to love themselves, which can help a lot in mastering that kind of love as you meet people by yourself.

What I mean by that is to keep it simple and allow your every day to be the best picture of how loving yourself first can very much improve your life.

Chapter Eight

ARE YOU STILL WITH ME?

Okay, we're going to give some more thought to life as we age. Why is it that in some other countries, seniors live to be one hundred years old or older? I think it's because they eat healthy, discover the importance of exercising daily, sleep a good seven to eight hours a night, and stay connected with friends of all ages and activities while always having that happy, peaceful spirit. Now that you're well adjusted in life, what are your thoughts? How would you answer this question?

Come on, now, open up and give us your opinion or thoughts on this. First, think to yourself: do you wake up feeling that spirit of being blessed all because you got up to see a new day? Uh-huh—tell the truth, because we are all listening to that thought.

I know that we all look at life differently as we get older. I had a thought. When I was younger and getting blood work, we never paid any attention to what was written down other than what the doctor shared with us.

And while on that note, I wish I had been more interested in my blood work when I was young so that I could have been more accountable about my numbers.

Now, when the doctor reads your blood work, he tells you about how bad your cholesterol and kidneys are and how you most likely will have to get on cholesterol medicine, and to hear that your kidneys have taken a bad turn is never good news. If I had known how important numbers were when I was young, maybe I could have been able to better monitor my state of well-being.

Yes, that's all well and good, because now that we know and are trying to relate this information to the young generations, it doesn't mean a thing or ring a bell to them that being on the right track while you're young can really help you as you grow older.

2024 is the new year for many of us to possibly find out some bad news about our health, and for some others, it continues to get better and better. Why? We want to live a long time and have something to contribute to our family and society as a whole. But in no way can you give up, even though it can be a challenge. Keep moving toward a healthy life.

I cannot state this more clearly: young people should try to stay transparent about what is going on with their health at all their appointments.

It is so important to know your numbers and what those medical terms mean. Stay focused on knowing your numbers and what they mean. As you wait for the doctor to get back, you do your own research. If you own a computer, use it. I am addressing this to those over fifty who are realizing that things are going downhill with their health.

Earlier in my story, I indicated that I have tremors and have opted out of taking any kind of medicine. Why? Okay, as I said before, this is my story, so the reason I opted out was that there's always that chance of something else breaking down. My theory is that every time you are placed on some kind of medication, whether blood pressure, cholesterol, gout, or whatever, it may help with that problem, but it creates a new one.

Why can't someone find a way for us to eat healthy foods, meaning fruit, healthy protein, and vegetables, to support our health instead of always shooting for all these different kinds of pills that are so harmful for our bodies?

Why? Wouldn't it be nice if our doctors could prescribe beets, spinach, celery, and cucumber juicing to boost our iron deficiencies and pineapple, orange, ginger, and lemon juicing for vitamin D deficiencies?

I would love to have a written prescription indicating the type of fruits or veggies to be taken for a certain length of time to better build our immunity and completely put the pharmaceutical industry out of business. My guess is that when a person is admitted to the hospital with an illness, they are given foods that they shouldn't be eating.

I remember the last time I went to the emergency room; it was back in 2013, when I complained about numbness in my left arm and pain in my chest. The doctor thought that maybe I had had a stroke in my sleep, so I was admitted. When I got to my room, which I shared with a person who had just had a heart attack and was recovering, she introduced herself and said I better take a look at the menu and order something, and that they had just finished serving the last meal of the day.

She said, "They make the best roast beef, and their grill cheese sandwiches are very good. And can you fill out that form at your table and dial for food service?"

Why isn't there such a thing as having a diabetic chef, a cancer chef, or chefs who are educated to prepare special meals? For all hospitalized patients with underlying illnesses that are suffering, it is unspeakably sad and senseless. A person who is in the hospital for cancer should not be eating meat, dairy, sweets, bread, or carbs; none of that should be on their menu.

Again, I'm not a doctor, but common sense would tell me to try a plant-based or raw-juice-based special diet in order to help their healing process recover. Along with learning how to eat and heal by way of juicing for a time that will be healthy for them to process, that person should be eating a healthy, liquid-filled meal that keeps them and their vital signs on a good note. However, who am I to judge? It seems like a sensible healing approach to me, even though I'm not a doctor.

A few years ago, a friend of a friend's daughter never thought that it was important for her to follow through and get her colonoscopy. You see, she never had time; she was always so busy with her shop, and when she did, the feedback from the test was not in her favor.

She later got some news from her doctor showing that the test showed that she had stage 4 colon cancer.

She was only forty-eight years old, and all her life she had eaten unhealthy fast foods. For once in her life, she had asked her parents if they would help her start juicing and find a better way to conquer the thought of maybe dying real soon. Neither one of her parents knew anything about juicing and would not go along with their daughter's idea because they too were always busy, so they continued to provide her favorite fried foods, meats, sweets, breads, and carbs; that was not healthy for her to consume. Again, that's just common sense. What are your thoughts about that? Do you honestly feel at times that you have to explain yourself to people along your journey as you age because of your visible appearance? Do you need to give people an explanation about something you have or whatever you're going through?

Understanding that I have essential tremors that really have nothing to do with anyone's concern, I've gotten to be my own cheerleader. I have good days and bad days, but my motto has always been "I couldn't be better."

What I'm trying to share here is that one day, a dear friend of mine gave me a call to see if I would like to check out this new restaurant that just opened up.

She wanted me to meet her sister, who would be visiting Arizona for the first time in twelve years. "Yes, please bring her along; I'd really like to meet her," I insisted. As I was waiting in the car, she managed to park a few cars down. I got out of the car and saw Delores giving me a hand wave to acknowledge her presence.

I noticed that her sister seemed to be much older than her, although this was my first time even knowing that she had a sibling. We stopped for a moment to introduce ourselves, and at first Gertrude seemed to be a bit feisty and outspoken as she looked inside her purse to find that her smartphone had been left behind. No way was this going to have a chance to put a damper on this beautiful, sunny day.

As we walked into the restaurant, there was a hostess who seated us at a booth. As we walked over to be seated, we heard a voice say, "I would like to be seated at a table." And yes! That was the voice of Gertrude; she then pointed to a table with four chairs, indicating that she never puts her purse or bags on the floor of any restaurant. Have you ever met someone and known right away that they made you feel very uncomfortable in their presence? Yes!

Maybe it was a bad idea to agree to go on a lunch date with her sister. How would you have handled this situation?

Lunch for me has always been soup and a small salad, or a cup of soup and a half sandwich. So I chose to have the healthy chicken soup with roasted sweet potatoes, mushrooms, and kale, along with a healthy salad.

The sisters went on to order entrees. So we all started to sit quietly for a minute, and then I said, "Gertrude, so far, how are you finding your stay here in Arizona?"

Well, she said, "First thing, it's a bit too hot for me." I then said, "Maybe next time you come to visit your sister, you may want to come during the fall season; we have very nice weather here during that time." Just then, my big bowl of soup arrived. Wow, it was so meaty and brothy and looked so deliciously good.

However, while everyone else was waiting for their entrees, Gertrude seemed to be staring at me very hard and saw that my head was bobbing in a "yes" position and my hand was trembling as I was eating the broth from my delicious soup. "Oh," she said, "do you have Parkinson's?"

Delores then gave Gertrude a menacing glance that seemed to be saying, "Mind your own business." Gertrude then revealed herself, saying, "I'm eighty-two years old, and I've never met anyone with Parkinson's." When she said that to me, I had to take a deep breath and take a few seconds, and at the same time, I think my anxiety had reached a high level that I was feeling for the first time. I'd never had anyone ask if I had Parkinson's disease. "What's your age?" Was her subsequent inquiry. In response, I said, "I'm seventy-five years old, and I don't have Parkinson's disease. Instead, I have essential tremors, or ET, which I've had since I was fifty-two years old, but for some reason, as I've aged, it has gotten a bit worse."

Gertrude then said, "I'm so sorry; I know that must be a difficult challenge for you. Will you be all right trying to sip your broth?"

"Yes, Ma'am, I will." That was my response to Gertrude. Some people just don't get it. No matter how old you are, there is always someone who will get your goat or have something to say about you, whether you know them or not. To simplify what I'm saying, do you believe that as we get older, that childlike grudge or attitude never leaves your spirit and that you are built with that conception all through the rest of your life?

And to my readers, how would you have dealt with this situation? I will always believe that as we grow older, we put away childish things and mannerisms and move forward to gain some kind of wisdom.

I sensed from the beginning that Gertrude would be hurtful to me, but I never imagined that she would look at me so intensely to make me ponder.

I now feel compelled to introduce myself and my ET to any new friends I make as a result of this encounter. How would you have handled this situation? What would you have done? And how would you have felt? Lastly, would Gertrude's words have intimidated you at any length? Think about it for a minute.

Chapter Nine

HOW CAN WE BOOST OUR ENERGY?

Just because we lose sight of some things in life, that doesn't take away from the choices that we make on a day-to-day basis. Choices are what we now have more of, as we finally have freedom now that we're fully retired. Say it: "I'm free now that I am fully retired."

Now *energy* is known as the capacity or power to do work; that being said, as we awaken every day to begin a productive way of living our lives that requires energy, like clockwork, we should find an exercise that works for us and allows us to stay on track with it on a daily schedule.

There are so many seniors out there who are energized to do mountain climbing, swimming cross country, golfing, being good tennis players, and so many other things.

Did you forget that there's a whole world out there waiting for something big for you to do or make happen? Maybe you're one of those people who enjoy traveling, journaling, and sharing vivid pictures of what they see in order to allow others to see a brighter picture.

The whole point is that those eighty and over are doing a lot better than others below their age. I guess it depends on what you are stuck with in light of keeping things real in your active life and continuing to keep going, because you know that it's up to you and that you always believed in yourself. And become your own hero in all matters of your life.

For all of those people, I stand up and give them all applause for their energy levels and the success that they continue to achieve.

Being able to inhale the freshness in the light of a new day is amazing when you think about how wonderful it is to awaken and be alive to see yet another beautiful day of trying new things. I know a longtime friend who started a club for sixty-five-year-olds and older. In fact, she is a travel agent who does some work on the side helping seniors to find ways to have some daytime adventures.

Ida is seventy-two and enjoys finding trips for those seniors who love to travel, but being with groups that allow them to feel comfortable and excited gives them the chance to meet other seniors as well. I really like the idea of being able to take train excursions with maybe an overnight stay at a nice hotel or lodge for one night.

I would love to join, but Ida's club is on the east coast, five and a half hours away by plane.

Pickleball seems to be the new way of having fun these days among many seniors. I enjoyed playing pickleball with my family and friends. You really can get a good workout. I never tried to play golf, although people in Arizona play it every single day, without a doubt. I don't know—I have never been interested in that sport, but I admire and respect those who are strong players.

On a cool day, I enjoy taking long walks and listening to myself and what I have to say while strolling all by myself. It doesn't bother me at all to walk alone, because my mind converses with my brain, and I sense that it may be clearing out old debris that is hidden and needs to be thrown out. And yes, maybe this is not a good clarification of what I'm trying to say, but I just want you to think it over.

Can you understand that as I continue to share my story, it's okay for you to think about your own? I'm sure that you have a lot to say about things that have happened in your life—all those "woulda"s, "shoulda"s, and "coulda"s and the effects they had on you. Were they at all hurtful?

It took some time to figure out that some of those past situations were hurtful or not right.

Some things in life have generated different lasting imprints on all of us, leaving us with a bandage or cover to secure those wounds and the scars that we could not forget, but we came through like a champ after all those challenges. And as we have aged, they have become our past experiences that we learned from to get this far; now we share with others how we got to where we are now.

Am I right? I can see your smiles, as you can appreciate the fact that you can say, "I've been there, and I've done that" and truly know where that person has gone who is now going in a much better direction.

But you know what? You got through, didn't you? Yes, you did, because what didn't break you made you stronger. And that is the truth. I'm so sure that these days you have been filled with so much love, peace, and comfort in knowing what you went through and coming out feeling so proud of those challenges that helped to make you a better person.

Believe me, there has never been a living being who has never been without challenges from their childhood into their adult life.

For one reason or another, I have dealt with challenges that have been a struggle to conquer.

You had to believe that those things would turn around and you could find a way out of the situation, and later you learned that results were real and there is always a solution to every problem.

Sometimes you couldn't resolve your situation right away, but it took some time to figure it out, and you got through it. Everything in life is fixable and can work in your favor as long as you have patience and time to get it resolved.

Keep in mind, too, that nothing in life lasts forever. But some things are repairable according to how you take care of them for the life of the items. As for those people in your past who may have hurt you, would you want to salvage those friendships? How would you answer that question? Maybe you need a moment to think about it.

You can surely remember the things that happened to you that you thought were impossible to fix or resolve. After some time has passed, you realize that there is a solution to every problem and that it may not be as bad as you think. And nine times out of ten, it's not even a problem.

I know that as we get older, we focus on our ability to have learned and gained so much throughout our lifetime.

In many ways, we forget that our brains have generated an archive or storage room where all that memorabilia finds space on a shelf in your mind as a collection of things that you have experienced and accomplished as you lived your life throughout those wonder years. We can boost our energy levels by staying very much in the present and ceasing to stay within our own space.

There are those who wish to keep to themselves because they are getting older, claiming that they are just not interested in keeping up with everyday things. But in life, it has made sense for all of us to keep going. I remember the time back in the day when I was married, and as my husband and I slowly entered into our fifties, he would always tell me that if he ever stopped working, he would die.

As for myself going through a divorce, that was when I thought I would die. And yet neither one of us left this earth, all because death doesn't come that easily. Yes, going through my divorce at the healthy age of fifty-one really did take a toll on my health. Can you guess why and how?

Let me say this: I allowed it to take over all my energy, causing me to lose hope, to not take the best care of myself, and to focus on being alone. Sure, I put on a lot of weight, thinking that I would never find anyone else to be close or comparable to what I just lost. I wish I knew then what I know now about life, but I chalk it all up to experiences and mistakes along the way. Sometimes we have to go through things in order to be able to come out of them and say, "I was able to get through it."

We all know that life is about living and learning, even as we make mistakes along the way. Tell me about it. What have you gone through that took you to another place in life that allowed you to get through okay?

Chapter Ten

WHEN THINGS GET COMPLICATED FOR YOU AS A SENIOR

How do you act when adhering to new things and learning about changes in your everyday vocabulary? Do you find that a bit complicated, or need I say more? I'm delighted when I think about how fortunate I am to be around my family while living in Arizona.

I haven't been a bit hesitant about asking for help in those times when I needed support. I remember when my daughter got me my first cellphone for my birthday and how upgrading my phone every so many years has allowed me to stay relevant by being able to move forward on a day-to-day basis and enjoy the different apps that are incorporated on my cell. I no longer find it difficult to understand, even with all the information on my cellphone.

My only brother, who passed away—may he rest in peace—would always say, "Sis, speak about what you know and learn more about what you don't know. In other words, that allows you to be safe, other than speaking about things you think you know something about."

So in writing this story, I will speak about my tremors; for some time now, things have been complicated for me with this browbeating form of disability. The shaking of my left hand has found a way to trouble my signature hand, the nodding of my head, and voice box as well.

Now tell me if that's not complicating things in my life. Tell me about it. Does that sound complicated to you? I enjoy my life as a senior, yet I often ask myself, "Why did I have to develop tremors?"

I've been dealing with this situation for over twenty years, so I guess what doesn't break me will actually make me stronger. So for now, I'm dealing with the idea that it comes with age. You see, I try not to make things complicated only because there's nothing I can do about it. Medication is totally out of the question; I was prescribed medication, but my body cannot tolerate it.

So I decided to take each day as it came and deal with it the best way I could by staying busy, being around loved ones, and enjoying life as a somewhat happy and excited human being. Life gives you back what you put out, and I'll say no more than that I'll try, as always, to only put out good to get good back in return.

So is your life worth it? Take good care of yourself and take a big interest in eating the good foods that would give you some kind of healing instead of medication.

Realistically, back in the primitive time, people would fast when getting sick only to detox from everything for days, to clean out their systems in order to begin again with preparing only good substances for their bodies. Sometimes the old methods work far better than these new modern-day methods for using all kinds of pharmaceutical brands that are overpriced and are not a sure cure in any way.

Power and money shape the kind of world we live in today. Anything can be brought only to have money and, yes, power. But as we get older, that's not what we, as seniors, are looking to achieve in our later days.

Whether you try to believe it or not, life gives us a margin of activities to develop into a mainstream of possibilities. As I will continue to repeat again and again, as retirees, we have so much time allotted to start thinking outside the big box. By that, I simply mean get up, move about, be creative, and meet people at your nearest senior centers. Apply for part-time work in your area or even do some volunteer work so that you can be on a schedule within a time frame. Humble yourself to help others with some light work around their home, or even adopt a pet for company. Having someone to look after is, at best, rewarding. Maybe at the end of your day, you'd like to start a journal and later turn it into a self-published work. Learn to paint; there are classes everywhere.

It's all about taking care of your health and being happy every single day, along with having a good spirit. Some might see this as almost impossible—especially when everyone's health is not always in tip-top condition to be that kind of happy. Okay? I can understand that, because I do have some bad days, but my good days override anything that could make me feel that my day is not going to be good. You know that feeling when you bump your toe first thing in the morning? You will likely believe that this is a sign of the beginning of a bad day. How true that has been for a lot of us, but you have to learn to change that scenario and start thinking, "I couldn't be better" and believe that you are at your best.

Life is not promised; only if we take care of ourselves do we see longevity.

I think the most important things about our health are the brain, the gut, and exercising on a daily basis. Keeping your brain motivated to work can be a task as we get older. However, life doesn't slow down because we stop thinking. Being in the state of knowing what comes next can make things a bit complicated. So read and find ways to use your mind in order to stay mentally relevant.

Are you still with me? By now, I hope I'm not repeating myself or not making sense; if so, please take a moment to catch up. I do believe that writing is my safe haven, as a fact, all because when I write and get an idea to speak about something, it allows me to keep it moving, because, at a certain point, I might forget what I'm trying to say.

Can you remember how back in the day, when you were growing up, it was so rude to talk over or jump into someone's conversation? It's funny how, at my age now, I seem to talk over and jump into conversations when I can before I lose that thought. Becoming forgetful is no joke; at times you feel lost and out of the picture as you try hard to stay relevant as a participant in the conversation.

I just don't know sometimes how, as we get older, we slowly find ourselves declining in the ability to stay on top of things like trying to remember. But still, life continues to go on, whether you come along or not. The good thing about all this is that we will get through it as we continue to encounter these challenges to the best of our ability.

But I allow myself to take a minute to backtrack and get it right, in order to keep things real in my story. As I said before, we age by the minute, not by the day, and I do believe that's how it goes.

You see, the dictionary describes the brain as the most complex part of the human body. The three-pound organ is the seat of intelligence, interpreter of the senses, initiator of body movement, and controller of behavior. Lying in its bony shell and washed by protective fluid, the brain is the source of all the qualities that define our humanity.

But we already know that our brain controls our thoughts, memory, emotions, touch, motor skills, vision, breathing, temperature, hunger, and every other process that regulates our body.

Just as the brain has a job to do, we have to make it our job to keep finding exciting, positive, and productive things to live up to for our brains to stay relevant and stay strong.

Finding ways like cooking, creating, and using our thought patterns to keep the brain alive and motivated to not go dormant and become lost or in a state of dismay, how many of us keep God first in everything we set out to do or accomplish?

I know that I shouldn't have to break this to you this way, because without ever having to say this, I do know that we all take time out to pray in our daily lives. Because prayer has always been the lift in our spirits that allows us to wake up each day with laughter in our hearts. Tell me, What's your opinion on that, if I may ask?

I remember a dear friend who had just turned eighty-seven. She lived alone and always took good care of herself until one day, when I visited her, she said a strange thing had happened to her. It happened one day as she headed out and got into her car. All of a sudden, she forgot where she was going; she stopped right in the middle of traffic.

Her brain went completely blank. Good thing there wasn't any traffic in her lane, which allowed her to be safe.

But suppose there had been a lot of traffic out there? Could you imagine what would've happened if there was? After gaining her composure, she found her way back home, but unfortunately, she did have an accident that almost totaled her car as she ran into a wall, all because, as she said, her mind went blank.

I had known this friend for many years; she was sharp, smart, and very well adjusted to her everyday life and schedules. I really couldn't understand what had taken place that day. So at eighty-seven, losing her means of transportation broke her heart, because she went everywhere in her car: doctor appointments, the market, Bible studies, visiting her friends, and Sunday services. Now that she doesn't have a car, it is impossible for her to attend her church service on Sundays, Bible studies on Wednesdays, her shopping along with her daily routine, as well as her doctor's appointments.

So that was when I decided to help her out and suggested that my gentleman friend and I would come by and drop her off at Sunday service, but on that Sunday morning, as we pulled up into her driveway, there was no one waiting.

So I gave her a call on my cell, and she answered by saying, "Someone came into the house late last night and stole my underwear, and they turned over my trash. I think I better not go to service today." Before hanging up the call, I asked if I could come inside to see if she was alright. When she let me in, I noticed that her glass door to her stove was cracked and in need of repair.

That was when she addressed another issue: that someone had come in her house knocked over her trash, and took her trash can. I took a side eye as I thought to myself, this is strange. I wonder what really happened here.

Right then, I knew that something was not right and proceeded to go outside and tell my gentleman friend, who was waiting in the car for both of us to come out for church. My gentleman friend knew instantly that my friend was suffering from dementia. And that was when he said to me, "That was not a good sign; your friend needs to call her son."

So with all of that being said, at sixty-two years old, that was my first experience trying to understand some simple signs of dementia. God help us when we all may have to see signs of that sort of performance in ourselves.

I am not trying to dismiss the topic of God, the Most High, or even the Universe, but I would think that you would agree that God is the way, the truth, and the light that guides our spirit on a daily basis. Whether our minds stay relevant or not, we can always find room in our brains to say a prayer or two of thanksgiving and gratitude. What do you think?

My dear friend who developed dementia read her Bible every single day, went to Bible study every Wednesday evening, and went to church on Sundays to fellowship. She even sang in the choir; her voice was like an angel at eighty-seven, but unfortunately, she started forgetting things and losing her way, and her son took her away to never be seen or heard from again.

Mrs. Jasmine was her name. I never heard from her again; she was truly a dear friend we had met at church when she was seventy, and she never looked over fifty years old. I wish you could have met this beautiful person; her spirit was so full of grace.

I'm sure you would have loved her as a dear friend as well. Whenever I pray, I always ask for spiritual growth. Yes! I do believe that we need to have a God in our lives to help massage our spiritual well-being. Think about it.

Mrs. Jasmine's spirit gave me so much light to see my way at times because of her spiritual character as a person.

She was a God-fearing, happy person who showed kindness to all those who crossed her path, even after she developed dementia. I do believe that prayer and knowing a higher being keep our spirits cleansed.

Chapter Eleven

YES, I AM STILL THRIVING HIGH

Do you ever feel as though you are not even here and that you have lost your will to thrive? To tell the truth, I really haven't had time to think about that. Five years ago, my immediate family encouraged me to think about moving to Arizona to enjoy a better quality of life, as the weather is never too cold and the sun is shining every day.

So I took them up on that offer and decided to take the leap to meet people around my age, along with finding a passion to enjoy every day. I must say that it has really been a pleasure living with my family and keeping busy at seventy-six years old. We have learned to take care of each other, and at the same time, we have grown to love and respect everyone's opinions. Every day has been a grand moment in my life. I enjoy the time we put into playing pickleball twice a week.

Don't get me wrong, I still want my forever home to be a smaller place, of course. During the pandemic, we were able to budget and save for one day owning our own forever dream home.

We all have been following our passions in making money moves and saving as much as we can as we await the right time. So do I ever feel alone?

Well, to be perfectly honest with you all, yes, I do miss a lot of my friends who have passed on, and I deeply miss my furry grandbaby boy cat, Zephaniah, who passed away last year at seventeen years old. Lastly, I miss the east coast and some old friends there, along with the many attractions and the eateries. But I can always make time to go back and visit, which is good. Tell me, what do you miss? Do you find that you are all alone at times?

The other day, when I got up, I looked in the mirror and began to criticize my appearance. Have you ever done that to yourself? I know we try to be kind to ourselves; however, that can be so hard to do. While washing my face, I noticed that my eyes were getting smaller, and while brushing my teeth, I saw very clearly that my teeth were getting yellow.

I like to think that I'm still beautiful, but as we grow older, everything, I guess, has to suffer as well. What do you think about that? No pun intended, but getting old can be very interesting at times because you find that something new has stopped by in your aging life.

I enjoy the fact that age is just a number, but you do feel that number rising in your life and making it hard sometimes to do certain things in your aging life.

Getting back to maybe feeling alone, I know that throughout our lives, some of our best friends, as well as those friends we meet along the way, will disappear. The camaraderie of trust, love, and conversations is no longer there to embrace. Because of the circle of friends we lose in our lives, the Lord knows that we will all find our way to leave this earth at the end of life's journey. So I say, let's quietly put aside those thoughts of feeling and being lonely and embrace the fact that we are still here and there is still so much more to do even as we grow older each day.

I never put down anyone who is struggling to do more and can't. I would only suggest getting a tape recorder and telling your story. Start sharing your amazing story; we all have wonderful stories to share.

You know, the other day I saw a movie on *Twilight Zone*, and the title was "Kick the Can." It was so memorable only because one of the characters named Charlie was waiting for his son to pick him up from the senior home he resided in; later when his son arrived Charlie was so disappointed, because he thought he would be leaving his place where there were senior people who chose not to be active only because everyone there kept saying they were too old to do anything. But Charlie thought differently. One night he decided to wake up Ben and some other senior friends to go outside and play kick the can, and poor Ben simply said, "I'm too old to do those things any more," but Charlie believed otherwise. So the seven seniors snuck out to play, and would you believe it? Their imagination was so strong that they all became children again. Ben could only cry out and say, "Charlie, take me with you. I want to go along with you and kick the can too. I want to be active and childlike and not sit around in this old folks' home."

To me, the moral of the story says so much: yes, we all have gotten older in years, but always consider yourself as old as you may feel. Never give up enjoying some activities in your life, because that's what gives you the good graces to have the childlike innocence to enjoy your life no matter what age. I love watching *Outer Limits* and *Twilight Zone.* I began watching those shows when I was a kid, and now I find that I can understand them a lot better.

Even back then, those stories could sometimes be so surreal, breaking down everyday life in a slightly scary way. We may not understanding something when we are young, but it can become much clearer as we get older.

I must say that I have a deep interest in loving the old movies; they have become much more meaningful as you follow the story. They are classy and stylish, even elegant, as the women and men in those old movies back then were more laid-back and respectful and nothing like today's movies.

It's always a disadvantage when the TV shows now leave nothing to the imagination; everything comes off, and you see every part of the anatomy. But I can say that doesn't bother me, because I always have the option to change the channel. Is that what you choose to do?

I think I'll take a break now and call it a day, and I hope you all are not getting too tired of listening to my story. It has truly been a pleasure checking in with all of you, readers. Do you have any plans for today, tomorrow, next week, and next month? Are you able to think ahead? Look, life is living, and it doesn't wait for anyone to answer; it wants you to do whatever is there for you to do.

Let us not forget that life is for the living. I cannot express enough how being retired allows so much freedom for space in your life to get excited and embrace all kinds of things as a living human being. Need I say anything else other than get up and do your thing, challenge life by living and enjoying what's out there, and embrace the light of day as it comes with new adventures.

And lastly, I know it's hard to stay on track for all those out there who feel the anxiety of feeling lost and nonexistent in the world, especially when you have that feeling of being at death's door. Find a quiet place and take a seat. Now inhale slowly from your stomach up; then let it out through your nose. Try doing this at least ten times or more times as needed. Close your eyes while doing this exercise, and only think about those wonderful moments in your life that have made you happy. And pour into the Universe some calming affirmations to replenish and rebuild your spirit while you picture all that goodness. As you speak to the Universe, listen, understand, and believe in what you are saying: "I am healthy, I am healed, I am whole, I am beautiful, and I am strong.

And allow your body to take on its own method of healing power to continue to work as it should, giving you a much clearer mindset so that you know that you will be just fine. I am so thankful and happy that life has me getting better every day and moving forward with positive thoughts.

And life will go on to stimulate your existence. Believe me, it really does work once you develop the right mindset.

Start out each day by saying, "I couldn't be better." Be that senior star that shines so brightly for others to see as a torch of gratitude as you age.

As we get older, we turn into more knowledgeable people who have always been instructors and listeners, along with being role models.

We have imagination, determination, and persistence.

Family unity is the oldest title that we uphold.

We combine the strength of age with knowledge.

In closing, let me share this idea with you: a senior is someone who is older than others by a certain number of years, typically as a result of having lived a longer life, and who consequently possesses a higher status or standing than others, particularly by virtue of holding the title of being the oldest person in the room.

A SALUTE TO SENIORS

If you don't have a story to tell, what has your life been about? My belief is that when we were born into the world, we had no idea that God had a book with blank pages with all our names on it; nonetheless, from that point forward, our life stories were recorded. How wonderful it would be if we could change things in that book such that each chapter of our stories had a satisfying conclusion. Making notes for each chapter that are relevant and practical in your life depends on how you live your daily life.

Every action we take has a purpose in life, but you try to pray, then pray some more, until you find the inner spiritual light that shines the brightest to guide you and light your way. When that light appears, you understand it was a lesson learned, and life moves on. We realize that God occasionally puts us through the greatest test of all, even as we age, to push through life in order to persevere. Finally, you will discover how to love unconditionally so that your light can continue to shine.

God's grace provides you with the ability to love, to grow, to have a solid foundation, and to have powerful healing qualities that enable you to overcome and triumph over all challenges.

Because of what you have learned by your experiences, you may not recognize how it can motivate others or how it has strengthened you to realize how courageous, heroic, and strong you have become in getting there. Instead, conquering challenges becomes your strength as you move forward, as we all grow older spiritually, mentally, and physically in a world filled with loving human beings.

I am so grateful for the love and support I have received from everyone who took the time to read my story.

I hope it was inspiring and encouraging.
If someone were to ask, “How do you feel today?”
answer, “I couldn’t be better.”

Here's my thought: Be as sharp as a pencil point and write your story; embrace the fact that you do have something to say, we all have wonderful stories to tell. Keep in mind that storytelling teaches us about life, ourselves and family. It becomes the gateway that draws us closer together.

www.ingramcontent.com/pod-product-compliance
Lightning Source LLC
LaVergne TN
LVHW041044150826
845672LV00001B/466
* 9 7 9 8 2 1 8 3 2 0 0 3 4 *